THE FIRST SETTLER OF THE NEW WORLD

THE FIRST SETTLER OF THE NEW WORLD

THE VINLAND EXPEDITION OF THORFINN KARLSEFNI

Jónas Kristjánsson

Vinland, or as the Norsemen delighted to call it "Wineland the Good," is really the northern section of Newfoundland.

W.A. Munn 1914

*This book is published with support from
the Icelandic Cultural Fund*

University of Iceland Press
Reykjavík 2005

© Jónas Kristjánsson 2005

Photographs: Gunnlaugur Jónasson, Kristján Jónasson and Þórður Ingi Guðjónsson
Maps: Gunnlaugur Jónasson
English translation and proofreading: Philip Roughton, Mary Sigurðsson and Kendra Willson
Cover design: Kristinn Gunnarsson
Layout: University of Iceland Press

Printed in Iceland by Gutenberg

All rights reserved. No part of this publication may be reproduced or used in any form or by any means without written permission of the publisher.

ISBN 9979-54-650-6

TABLE OF CONTENTS

A Short Exposition 7

The Settlement of Iceland and Greenland 8

The Sources on Vinland 12

Comparison of the two sagas 14
   1. Common features 14
   2. Divergent accounts 15
   3. Additional incidents in each saga 16
   4. Eirik's Saga more reliable 17

The route of Thorfinn Karlsefni 19
   Stone-Slab Land and Forest Land 19
   Vinland. Keel Point and Wonder Beaches 24
   Stream Bay and Stream Island 26
   Hop (Hóp) 27
   Back to Stream Bay. Expedition to the west coast 28
   Home to Iceland 29

Some Vinland questions 29
   Informants. Consonance and dissonance 29
   The discovery and exploration of Vinland 31
   Self-sown wheat 31
   Vines and grapes 33
   Chronology 36

L'Anse aux Meadows. Vinland today 39

In the wake of Thorfinn Karlsefni 46

Bibliography 51

A SHORT EXPOSITION

In recent years, the author of the present essay has been investigating the life of Gudrid Thorbjarnardottir and her husband Thorfinn Karlsefni, who in days of old made a great voyage to Vinland the Good with the intention of settling there. The story of this couple is told in particular in two Sagas of Icelanders, Eirik the Red's Saga (*Eiríks saga rauða*) and the Greenlanders' Saga (*Grænlendinga saga*). Unfortunately, Thorfinn and Gudrid were forced to retreat from Vinland back to Iceland after a few years' stay.

Various guesses have been made as to where Vinland was. My conclusion is that Karlsefni and his men tried to settle in the area which is today called Newfoundland. This is not a new hypothesis; artifacts from Nordic people who visited long ago have been found in the northernmost part of the province. However, my observations on Eirik's Saga suggest other locations further south in the province. In order to seek confirmation of this conclusion, I have made several journeys and explored the lay of the land. These investigations have strengthened my conviction, although no traces have yet been found of the habitation of these travelers in the area which I regard as most likely.

However, I feel it is worth taking the trouble to present my research for those who are curious to learn something about the ancient Vinland voyages. This piece is intended especially for the many Newfoundlanders who have assisted me and shown me hospitality and a warm reception on my research trips. They are now gathering forces to search for some of those artifacts which I am certain that Gudrid and Karlsefni left in Newfoundland a thousand years ago.

The settlement of Iceland and Greenland

Iceland is a young country in terms of the history of the Earth, formed gradually by lava eruptions that take place in the continental drift zone where the eastern and western plates meet. The climate is much milder than one would expect considering the northerly position of the country, because a warm ocean current reaches it, coming north from the Gulf of Mexico and spreading around the coastline. After the end of the last Ice Age the land slowly became covered in rich vegetation. Seals gathered along the coasts and birds by the thousands, and even millions, made their nests in the woodlands and on the cliffs. However, there were no land animals apart from the arctic fox, which was carried to the country on the pack ice that occasionally reaches the coast, causing cold weather and hardship.

Iceland was completely uninhabited for a long time before it was discovered by Norwegian Vikings late in the 9th century. At that time there was much unrest in Norway. The Norwegians were one of the most important seafaring nations in the world. Their merchant ships and longships were outstanding vessels, as can be witnessed by the replicas that were made in the 19th and 20th centuries and in which many voyages have been made. In the 9th century Viking voyages to Britain and Europe were at their peak, and the Vikings not only brought home provisions but also caused an increase in population and overcrowding within their homeland. King Harald Finehair was on the verge of bringing the whole country under his power, waging war on chieftains and minor kings. Many chose to flee from his domination, some to Viking settlements in England, Scotland and Ireland, others to the newly discovered land in the west which opened its generous arms to embrace the flow of immigrants from Norway. At this time Iceland had extensive birch woodland, between the mountains and the coast; the woods provided fuel and grazing for

From 1960-1970 the Norwegian couple Helge and Anne Stine Ingstad excavated old Nordic artifacts at L'Anse aux Meadows on the northern tip of Newfoundland. Afterward they delivered lectures and published books and articles on their research. Later the excavations and research there were continued by the Canadian government, primarily under the supervision of Birgitta Linderoth Wallace. A pleasant facility for research work and exhibitions was built on a hill overlooking the excavation site, and busts of the Ingstads were set up in front of the house. Replicas of several of the Nordic dwellings have been built a short distance from the raised outlines of the original dwellings' foundations. The artifacts at L'Anse aux Meadows were added to UNESCO's World Heritage List in 1978.

animals, and there was an abundance of salmon and trout in rivers and lakes and rich fishing grounds off the coast.

Records indicate that the settlement of Iceland lasted for a period of 60 years, from about 870 to 930. Nordic chieftains flocked to Iceland, most of them straight from their homeland but some from

Viking settlements in the British Isles where the clan had stayed temporarily. At the end of the settlement period, around 930, the new inhabitants founded an independent Icelandic state with a complete set of laws and parliament (Althing) for the entire nation. The Althing convened for two weeks each year at the place which has since become known as Thingvellir, situated just to the east of the present capital, Reykjavik. At the parliamentary sessions laws were modified, contracts made and judgements passed. In the beginning power was divided equally among 39 chieftains, who were called *goðar*, a derivation of the word *goð*, 'god,' since they were also in charge of the heathen religious sacrificial feasts.

The original and carefully planned Icelandic constitution proved its worth both in terms of results and longevity. The Icelandic Commonwealth or Free State lasted for almost three and a half centuries, and it nurtured a literary culture which was without parallel in northern Europe. The best known examples of this unique literature are the so-called sagas – fictionalized accounts of contemporary and past events, not only from Iceland, but also from other Viking countries, and especially from Norway, the mother country.

During the first centuries of settlement, the Icelanders still had a large fleet of ships in good condition, and the thirst for travel which had brought their fathers to the country still burned in their blood. They went even farther west in search of new lands. Eirik the Red, a man from Breidafjord in western Iceland, discovered a large country which he named Greenland, "and said that a good name would encourage people to move there," as Ari the Wise states in his *Íslendingabók* (Book of the Icelanders), the oldest and most trustworthy of the Icelandic historical sources, written c. 1130. Eirik's wish came true: in the years that followed, many people moved from Iceland to Greenland and established two settlements, both located on the southwest coast of the country. The settlements could rightly have been called "The Southern Settlement" and "The Northern Settlement," but according to common Icelandic usage they were

Replicas of ancient Nordic dwellings at L'Anse aux Meadows. The site receives numerous visitors each year, despite its isolated location.

named "The Eastern Settlement" and "The Western Settlement." Both settlements flourished in the first centuries, especially the Eastern Settlement, where Eirik the Red built his farmstead Brattahlid. Christianity came to Greenland, as it did to Iceland, about the year 1000. Churches were built in both settlements; a bishopric was founded, as well as a nunnery and a monastery. Ruins of stately buildings from as late as the end of the fourteenth century bear witness to prosperity and a flourishing culture.

In the late 13th century Greenland, along with its mother-country Iceland, submitted to the Norwegian crown; and at the end of the fourteenth century, all three countries came under the rule of Denmark. The ships of the Icelandic settlers had become worn out, and both Iceland and Greenland lacked the timber forests to make ocean-going vessels. This made the Greenlanders entirely dependent on the whims of foreign merchants for all of their imports. In Norwegian, and especially in Danish eyes, Greenland seemed endlessly far away. To sail out there was risky and often unprofitable. Finally Denmark completely lost sight of its colony, and all contact with Europe was broken for almost two hundred years. When explorers arrived in Greenland at the end of the 16th century, they found only the remains of collapsed farm buildings and worn wooden crosses standing above the bones of the ancient seafarers who had discovered America five centuries before the time of Columbus.

THE SOURCES ON VINLAND

1. The oldest record in which Vinland is mentioned is the History of the Bishops of Hamburg by Adam of Bremen, *Gesta Hammaburgensis Ecclesiae Pontificum*. There it states (in English translation):

> He (i.e. the king of the Danes) spoke also of yet another island of the many found in that ocean. It is called Vinland because vines producing excellent wine grow wild there. That unsown crops also abound on that island we have ascertained not from fabulous reports but from the trustworthy relation of the Danes. Beyond that island, he said, no habitable land is found in that ocean, but every place beyond is full of impenetrable ice and intense darkness. (Adam of Bremen 1959, p. 488.)

The Hamburg History by Adam was written shortly after 1070. The Nordic countries came under Adam's diocese and this work is one of the main sources on the history of the Nordic countries in the 10th and 11th centuries, even if some of it is exaggerated. His informant on the tale of Vinland, as well as on various other parts of the Hamburg History, was Sven Estridsson (Ulfsson), King of Denmark (d. 1080).

2. The next mention of Vinland is to be found in *Íslendingabók* of Ari the Wise around 1130, but unfortunately Vinland is only mentioned in passing. In his report on the discovery and settlement of Greenland, Ari includes this information:

"Both east and west in the country they found human habitations, fragments of skin boats and stone implements from which it was evident that the same kind of people had been there as inhabited Wineland and whom the Greenlanders called Skrellings." (The Book of the Icelanders 1930, p. 64.)

3. Ari names Vinland as though it were a well-known place, although voyages thither had long since ceased when he wrote his work. In the Icelandic annals from the year 1121 it says that Eirik Upsi, the bishop of Greenland, went to look for Vinland that year. (Islandske Annaler 1888, *passim.*) There are few records of Greenland from this time and nothing else is known about Bishop Eirik, nor is anything known about the outcome of the expedition.

4. The most detailed sources on the discovery of Vinland and the expeditions are two Icelandic sagas. One is called *The Saga of the Greenlanders* or *Greenlanders' Saga;* the other is called in one manuscript *Eirik the Red's Saga* and in the other *Thorfinn Karlsefni's Saga*. The latter name is more apt since Karlsefni is the protagonist of the saga, but the former name is more commonly used.

The events described in the two sagas took place about the year 1000 but the sagas were not written until the thirteenth century. In between there were two and a half centuries of oral tradition, giving plenty of time for forgetfulness, exaggeration and superstition to creep in. The two sagas show signs of having been written down independently of each other.

Comparison of the two sagas

A closer comparison of the two sagas shows partly overlapping narratives in both (of course with different wording) and partly divergent accounts of the same events, with different additional incidents in each saga.

1. Common features

a. Most of the persons are common to both sagas: Eirik the Red, his wife Thjodhild, his four children and two children-in-law, several settlers in Greenland, etc.

b. The seafarers discover three new lands to the southwest of Greenland to which they give the names *Helluland* (Stone-Slab Land), *Markland* (Forestland) and *Vinland* (Wineland).

c. Eirik's son Leif saves some shipwrecked people and from that deed he gains the nickname "the Lucky".

d. Thorstein Eiriksson marries Gudrid Thorbjarnardottir but he dies soon afterward from an epidemic.

e. The widow Gudrid remarries, this time with Thorfinn Karlsefni, a rich merchant from Skagafjord in North Iceland.

f. They travel to Vinland with many followers and intend to settle there, bringing with them "all kinds of livestock."

g. Their son Snorri is born there.

h. The natives at first have friendly dealings with the newcomers, but later fighting breaks out. Karlsefni's bull frightens the natives with its bellowing.

i. Because of the hostility of the natives and discord among the would-be settlers, Karlsefni decides to turn back to Greenland.

j. Karlsefni and Gudrid move from Greenland back home to Iceland, where they live as farmers in Skagafjord.

k. Three well-known Icelandic bishops who lived in the 12th century are descended from them.

2. *Divergent accounts*

Even if most of the the persons and many events are the same in the two sagas, the circumstances are often different and the roles of some of the protagonists have been changed. The most striking differences are the following:

a. According to Eirik's Saga, Vinland was discovered by Leif the Lucky, the son of Eirik the Red, on his way to bring Christianity to Greenland. According to Greenlanders' Saga, on the other hand, the discoverer was a certain Bjarni Herjolfsson, son of one of Eirik's followers but an otherwise unknown man. This obscure sailor is not likely to have been made up by oral storytellers or by the saga-author as the discoverer of Vinland. On the other hand, Leif's discovery of Vinland is closely connected to the coherent and in many ways credible description of Thorfinn Karlsefni's expedition as described in Eirik's Saga (cf. below). A possible explanation for this discrepancy is that both Bjarni and Leif independently discovered the new lands in the west – even though it is unlikely that they sailed there together as they so happily do on the Vinland map (one of the obvious arguments for this document's being a fake).

b. Other explorers then follow in the wake of the first discoverers: in Eirik's Saga it is Thorfinn Karlsefni; in the Greenlanders' Saga it is Leif the Lucky (a natural continuation consistent with the discoverer in each saga). Thus in Greenlanders' Saga the coherent account of Karlsefni's expedition as told in Eirik's Saga is split into two: the journey of Leif and the journey of Karlsefni himself.

c. In Greenlanders' Saga, Thorvald Eiriksson is killed by the natives in Vinland on an independent expedition from Greenland. According to Eirik's Saga, Thorvald is just one of Karlsefni's many followers in his great expedition – though he is eventually killed in Vinland by the natives as in the other saga.

3. Additional incidents in each saga

Eirik's Saga is considerably longer and more detailed than Greenlanders' Saga and accordingly there are many additional episodes. Some of them are unimportant, having possibly been added by the author for literary purposes. Other pieces of information, however, are more important and most probably originate in stories that were passed down orally. This applies not least to the account of Karlsefni's expedition to Vinland, the central theme of Eirik´s Saga. The relation of this journey is split in two in Greenlanders' Saga. The first part is virtually identical to Leif's Vinland journey as related in Greenlanders' Saga (cf. above), but the second part has a parallel account relating to Karlsefni himself in Greenlanders' Saga. In Eirik's Saga the narrative is coherent, more detailed and more informative.

Even though Greenlanders' Saga is much shorter than Eirik´s Saga there is considerable additional material which is likely to have its roots in fact. Three such items may be mentioned:

a. Eirik's Saga tells only of three Vinland expeditions conducted by: (1) Leif the Lucky, (2) Thorstein Eiriksson (an unsuccessful expedition) and (3) Thorfinn Karlsefni. But in Greenlanders' Saga six Vinland expeditions are recorded under the leadership of: (1) Bjarni Herjolfsson, (2) Leif the Lucky, (3) Thorvald Eiriksson, (4) Thorstein Eiriksson (unsuccessful), (5) Thorfinn Karlsefni and (6) Freydis Eiriksdottir.

b. Greenlanders' Saga has preserved the place-name *Leifsbúðir* (Leif's Camp) which is not found in Eiriks's Saga. This name indicates that Leif stayed in Vinland for the winter as told in Greenlanders' Saga, since he built a camp. But according to Eirik's Saga he paid only a short visit there, in which case he would not have needed to establish any Leifsbudir. This place-name is likely to be old – and Leif's Camp plays a considerable role in Greenlanders' Saga.

c. The fifth Vinland expedition, that of Freydis Eiriksdottir, is bound to have roots in tradition, even though it is only reported in Greenlanders´ Saga, as mentioned above. There may be several reasons why this expedition is not mentioned in Eirik´s Saga.

One could cite even more examples of the similarities and differences between the two sagas, as well as examples of the account of one saga being more detailed than that of the other, but I will let this suffice. Nor is it worth citing examples of superstition or description which most people today would consider highly unlikely.

4. Eirik's Saga more reliable

My comparison of the sagas has led me to the conclusion that in regard to the lives of Thorfinn Karlsefni and his wife Gudrid, Eirik's Saga is more reliable than Greenlanders' Saga, and I will now provide some arguments to support this conclusion.

a. Eirik's Saga deals more fully with the origins of Gudrid Thorbjarnardottir. There, her family history is clearly accounted for, while in Greenlanders' Saga she turns up unexpectedly on a skerry off Greenland and her father's name is only mentioned in passing. She had well-known and distinguished descendants, as already mentioned, among whom are three Icelandic bishops who lived in the 12th century. The oldest of these bishops was in fact the grandson of her son Snorri, who was born in Vinland. This bishop, Thorlak Runolfsson, was a keen scholar who appointed Ari the Wise to write *Íslendingabók*, one of the most important sources on the early history of Iceland. Undoubtedly such a man would have been well aware of the origins of his grandfather and great-grandmother.

b. The account of Karlsefni's journey to Vinland and his stay there fits well with the local conditions on the east coast of North America, as I will explain. Evidently this is in part the same account as that of the journey of Leif the Lucky to Vinland in Greenlanders' Saga. The common parts of these accounts form a continuous tale in Eirik's Saga, which is thus most likely closer to the truth.

c. When Karlsefni came to Iceland, "he came home to his farm at Reynines," the saga tells us (earlier we have learned that his father lived there). In Greenlanders' Saga it is not mentioned where Karlsefni's father lived nor where he stayed during his first winter in Iceland. But "in the

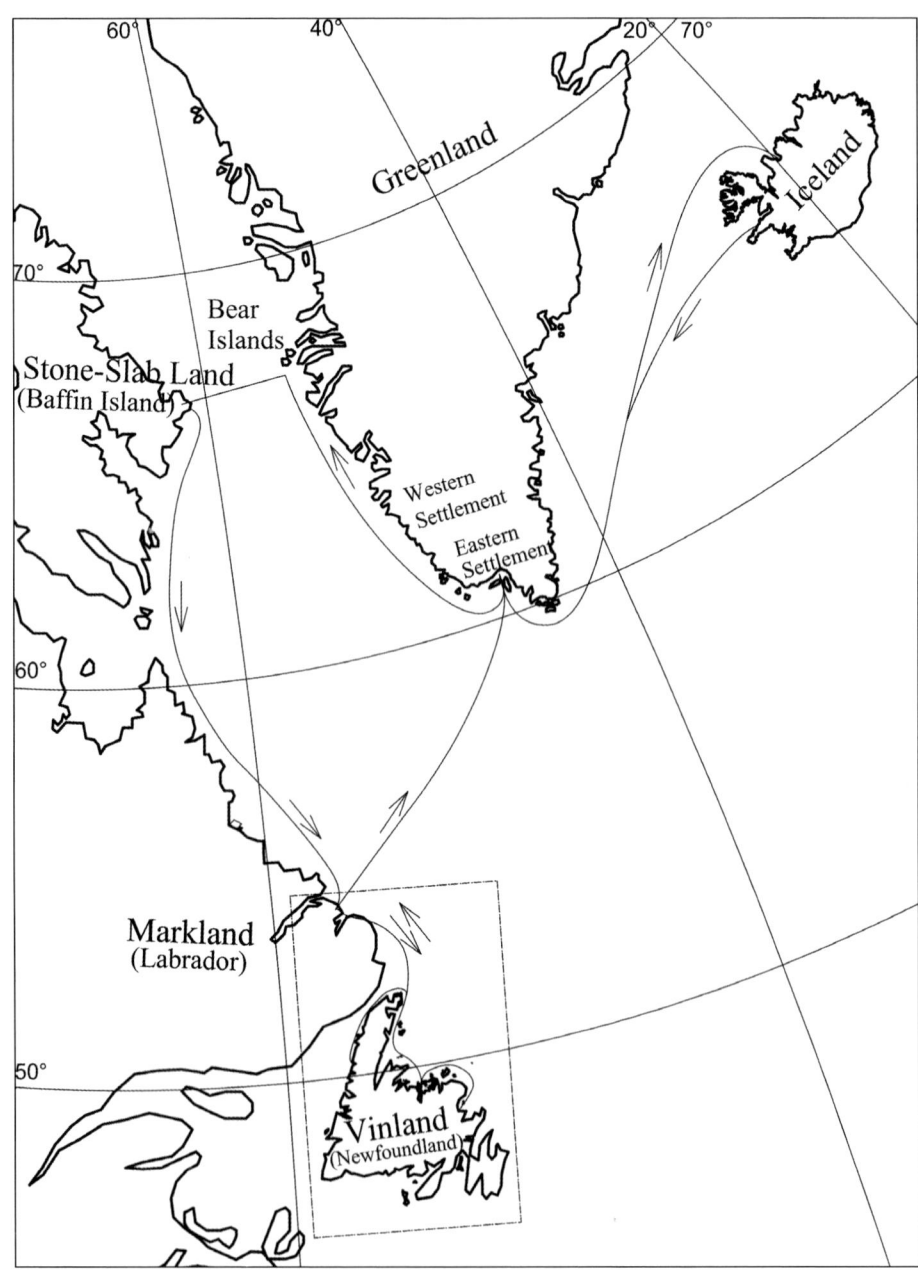

Thorfinn Karlsefni's route to Vinland at the start of the 11th century. He tried to keep land in sight so as not to lose his way, especially since previous explorers had gone astray "meandering around the sea" and never reached the promised land.

18

spring," the saga tells us, "he purchased the land at Glaumbær and established his farm there, where he lived for the remainder of his days." Scholars consider the account in Eirik's Saga to be more correct because the farm Reynines, later called Reynistadur, was associated with the descendants of Karlsefni in the 12th and 13th centuries.

d. At the end of Greenlanders' Saga, the last years of Gudrid Thorbjarnardottir's life are described with these words: "When Snorri married, Gudrid travelled abroad, made a pilgrimage south and returned to her son Snorri's farm. By then he had had a church built at Glaumbaer. Later Gudrid became a nun and anchoress, staying there for the remainder of her life."

It seems unlikely that there is any basis for this account. It should have taken place sometime in the third decade of the 11th century. Christianity had been declared the state religion by the Icelandic Parliament in the year 1000. It would most certainly have taken several decades for the new religion to become established to the extent of people undertaking pilgrimages to Rome, let alone for an old lady to become a "nun and anchoress." When such events are mentioned in the Icelandic sagas and are supposed to have taken place just after the year 1000, this is simply embellishment on the part of the writer to enable the person to depart from the world in a Christian manner. Christianity in Iceland finally became well-established when Iceland got its own bishop in 1056. The first reference to an Icelandic pilgrim which is considered to be true dates from the last years of his office. This pilgrim died in Denmark in 1073 on his way back from Rome. Gudrid's pilgrimage and her reclusive life are not mentioned in Eirik's Saga, which on this issue and on many others is more credible than Greenlanders' Saga.

THE ROUTE OF THORFINN KARLSEFNI

Stone-Slab Land and Forest Land.
The main part of Eirik's Saga and the part which has aroused most interest is the account of the expedition of Thorfinn Karlsefni and his followers to Vinland and their attempt to settle there. As mentioned

earlier, Karlsefni was an Icelandic farmer and merchant who sailed to Greenland shortly after the year 1000. He was accompanied by his cousin Snorri and also, on another ship, by two Icelandic merchants named Bjarni and Thorhall. Karlsefni stayed for the first winter at Brattahlid with Eirik the Red and married Gudrid Thorbjarnardottir, the widow of Eirik's son, Thorstein.

The wedding of Karlsefni and Gudrid would have taken place early in the year. "That winter there was much merrymaking in Brattahlid," the saga tells us, "many board games were played, there was storytelling and plenty of other entertainment to brighten the life of the household."

"There were great discussions of Snorri and Karlsefni setting sail for Vinland, and people talked about it at length. In the end Snorri and Karlsefni made their vessel ready, intending to sail in search of Vinland that summer. Bjarni and Thorhall decided to accompany them on the voyage, taking their own ship and their companions who had sailed with them on the voyage out." On the third ship were Thorvald, son of Eirik the Red, his sister Freydis and her husband Thorvard. "They had the ship which Thorbjorn [Gudrid's father] had brought to Greenland and set sail with Karlsefni and his group. Most of the men aboard were from Greenland."

"The crews of the three ships made a hundred plus forty men," the saga informs us. In the old language "a hundred" (*hundrað*) usually means 120. Accordingly, the participants in the expedition would have been 160 in all, a number which is probably greatly exaggerated. Such a crowd of people would have filled the three ships to overflowing, not least because, as we later learn, they also "brought all kind of livestock with them," because they intended to settle in Vinland. The number has swollen in the tradition or in the author's mind. (According to Greenlanders' Saga, Karlsefni had only one ship, and "he hired himself a crew of sixty men and five women"; also they "took all kinds of livestock with them." Such a cargo is even more improbable than that described in Eirik's Saga.)

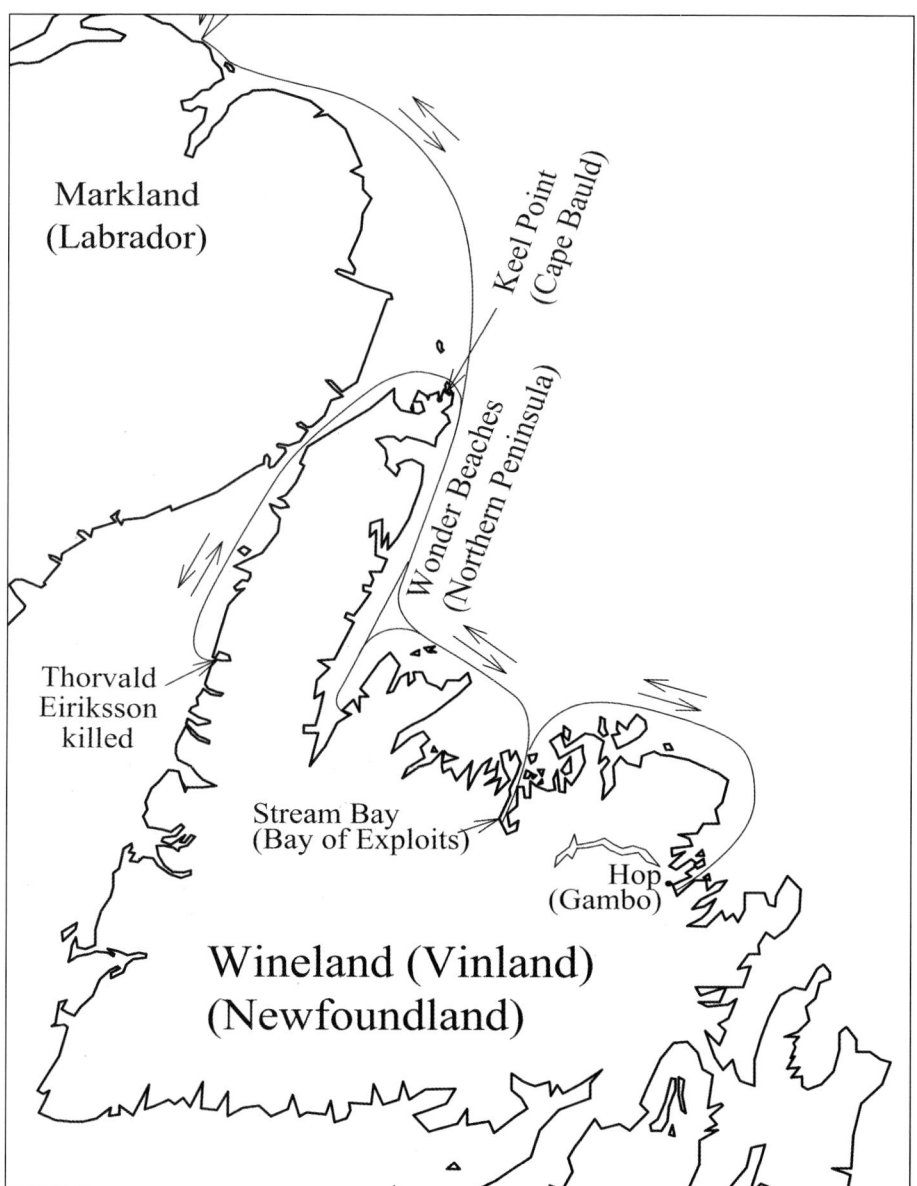

Thorfinn Karlsefni reached land in the west that he thought to be the same Vinland discovered by Leif Eiriksson, and spent three winters there. In the old Icelandic sagas some place-names in Vinland are given, and Jonas Kristjansson believes that he has discovered the actual locations of three of these: Kjalarnes (Keel Point), Furdustrandir (Wonder Beaches) and Hop.

Ring-headed pins used to fasten a cloak over the shoulders or at the neck have often been found buried in Scandinavia and Greenland. The Ingstads found this pin at L'Anse aux Meadows.

To begin with "they sailed along the coast to the Western Settlement, then past the Bear Islands with a northerly wind. After two days at sea they sighted land and rowed over in boats to explore it. There they found many flat slabs of stone (*hellur*), so large that two men could lie foot-to-foot across them. There were many foxes there. They gave the land the name *Helluland* (Stone-Slab Land)."

One manuscript refers to Bear Island (*Bjarney*, singular), and it was once thought that this was the same as today's Disco Island. However, in the manuscript of the saga which is now considered to be more reliable, the place is referred to in the plural, *Bjarneyjar*. Some scholars believe (quite plausibly) that this refers to islands off the west coast of Greenland facing Cape Dyer on Baffin Island, where the route across the Davis Strait is shortest.

Most scholars agree that Helluland must have been the same as

"After another two days passed [since their departure from Markland] they again sighted land and approached the shore where a peninsula jutted out. They sailed upwind along the coast, keeping the land on the starboard. There were large harbourless stretches, long beaches and sand flats... They gave the beaches the name Furdustrandir (Wonder Beaches) for their surprising length" (Eirik the Red's Saga).

Here is an aerial view of the desolate great Northern Peninsula of Newfoundland, which might have been the place called Furdustrandir by Nordic explorers. Winter snowdrifts remain on the Long Range Mountains at the end of May 2001. The photograph was taken from the aircraft window by Kristjan Jonasson, on the way to L'Anse aux Meadows from Springdale. In his journal Jonas Kristjansson wrote: "On the trip north we flew close by Furdustrandir, which I found to be an extremely eye-opening experience. For a great distance one sees cliffs and promontories along the sea, sheer and exposed. In one or two places the coastline is broken by bays and coves that cut into the land, and I was informed – in fact shown on maps – that there are human dwellings there in certain places."

modern Baffin Island. Obviously Karlsefni, afraid of getting lost on the open sea, followed the coastline as closely as possible. When the ancient Greenlanders went seal hunting to the so-called *Norðurseta*, far to the north of the two settlements, they might have sighted the mountains of Baffin Island.

"After that they sailed with a northerly wind for two days, and again sighted land, with large forests and many animals. An island lay to the south-east, off the coast, where they discovered a bear, and they called it *Bjarney* (Bear Island), and the forested land itself *Markland* (Forest Land)."

Modern scholars agree that Markland must have been some part of the coast of Labrador. According to Greenlanders' Saga the explorer (Leif in that saga) not only encountered a "flat and forested" land but he also "came across many beaches of white sand." This reference to white beaches has drawn the attention of researchers to beaches further south like those of Cape Porcupine or even all the way to Blanc Sablon, south of the Strait of Belle Isle. But in Eirik's Saga there is no mention of any white beaches, so if we follow this saga we may select any stretch of land on the east coast of Labrador after the forested area has been reached. Bjarney could then be one of the numerous islands to be found off the east coast of Labrador.

Vinland. Keel Point and Wonder Beaches.
"After another two days passed they again sighted land and approached the shore where a peninsula jutted out. They sailed upwind along the coast, keeping the land to starboard. There were large harbourless stretches, long beaches and sand flats. They rowed ashore in boats and, discovering the keel from a ship there, named the point *Kjalarnes* (Keel Point). They also gave the beaches the name *Furdustrandir* (Wonder Beaches) for their surprising length. After this the coastline was indented with numerous inlets which they skirted in their ships."

In all probability this new land was the same as modern Newfoundland. As one sails along the east coast of Labrador this land comes into sight straight ahead. To explain the name given to the northernmost peninsula in the saga one should probably turn to etymology. Kjalarnes is a common place-name in Iceland; the name is most likely derived from its shape. The saga's Keel Point would be

"Karlsefni headed south around the coast, with Snorri and Bjarni and the rest of their company. They sailed a long time, until they came to a river which flowed into a lake and from there into the sea. There were wide sandbars stretching out across the mouth of the river and they could only sail into the river at high tide. Karlsefni and his company sailed into the estuary and called the land Hop (Lagoon)... Every stream was teeming with fish. They dug trenches along the high-water mark, and when the tide ebbed there were halibut in them... The group had built their booths up above the water, with some of the huts farther inland, and others close to the shore" (Eirik the Red's Saga).

From Hop (now Gambo). The view in the photograph is toward the southeast, over the Gambo river and the wide plain on the opposite side of the river. The edge of Gambo Lake can be seen at the top.

the same as modern Cape Bauld, and Wonder Beaches would be the east coast of the Northern Peninsula. The description of that barren coast could scarcely be more fitting. Today the area is still mostly uninhabited and there is no road along the coast from south to north. From the west there is a single road across the peninsula to the isolated villages of Roddickton and Englee. Karlsefni would have had no wish to settle here.

When Karlsefni and his men had passed Furdustrandir, they put ashore a Scottish couple who were with them, "and told them to run southwards to explore the country and return before three days' time had elapsed." In due time they came back, "one of them with grapes in hand and the other with self-sown wheat." Obviously this is supposed to tell us that they had now reached the "Wine-land" discovered by Leif the Lucky.

Stream Bay and Stream Island.

The saga goes on: "They steered the ships into one fjord with an island near its mouth, where there were strong currents, and called the island *Straumsey* (Stream Island). There were so many birds there that they could hardly walk without stepping on eggs. They sailed up into the fjord, which they called *Straumsfjord* (Stream Bay), unloaded the cargo from the ships and began settling in.

"They had brought all sorts of livestock with them and explored the land and the resources. There were mountains there, and a pleasant landscape. They paid little attention to things other than exploring the land. The grass there grew tall.

"They spent the winter there and it was a harsh winter, for which they had made little preparation, and they grew short of food and caught nothing when hunting or fishing. They went out to the island, expecting to find some prey to hunt or food on the beaches. They found little food, but their livestock improved there . . . In the spring they moved further into Straumsfjord and lived on the produce of both shores of the fjord: hunting game inland, gathering eggs on the island and fishing at sea."

As before, the saga's description fits Newfoundland fairly well. But there are many fjords on the east coast and it is unclear which of them was Stream Bay. The most promising candidate seems to be the modern Bay of Exploits. Then Stream Island might be the same as Thwart Island. Another possibility is Halls Bay. The information that "there were mountains there" fits better with that place. There are also mountains in White Bay, the so-called Long Range Mountains. At the bottom of White Bay, Karlsefni might have discovered the first inviting places after passing Furdustrandir.

But we are investigating an extensive area and possible Viking house ruins would be difficult to discover. It is not unlikely that they could be buried under the buildings in one of the many modern villages.

Hop (Hóp).
"They then began to discuss and plan the continuation of their journey," the saga goes on. "Karlsefni wished to sail south and east along the shore, feeling the land would be more substantial the farther south it was, and he felt it was advisable to explore both.

"Karlsefni headed south around the coast, with Snorri and Bjarni and the rest of their company. They sailed a long time, until they came to a river which flowed into a lake and from there into the sea. There were wide sandbars stretching out across the mouth of the river and they could only sail into the river at high tide. Karlsefni and his company sailed into the estuary and called the land Hop. There they found fields of self-sown wheat in the low-lying areas and vines growing on the hills. Every stream was teeming with fish. They dug trenches along the high-water mark and when the tide ebbed there were halibut in them. There were a great number of deer of all kinds in the forest."

The description of Hop fits well with Gambo Pond, which is really a narrow lake about one kilometer wide and some thirty kilometers long. From this lake there flows a short and very shallow river, called Gambo Brook or Gambo River, into Freshwater Bay, which is an inlet from the great Bonavista Bay. An excellent salmon river called Mint Brook flows into the lake about one kilometer above the head of Gambo River.

Many scholars assume that Karlsefni and his followers took their ships into the lake and built their houses somewhere on its banks. Probably this assumption is based on the saga's later information that they "built their booths (viz. houses) up above the water (*upp frá vatninu*), with some of the huts farther inland, and others close to the shore." In this context the word *vatn* in Old Icelandic may mean either the "water" of the river, or that of the sea or of the lake. Actually the saga does not say that they brought their ships into the lake, only that they sailed "into the mouth of the river," and that they could "only sail into the river at high tide." It is most natural to suppose that they built their temporary houses on the banks of the river.

Back to Stream Bay. Expedition to the west coast.
Karlsefni and his company stayed at Hop for only one winter. Already in the first summer they had caught sight of some natives there, and in the spring many of those natives came rowing in hide-covered boats. At first, Karlsefni and his men traded happily with the visitors, but Karlsefni forbade the sale of swords and spears. The natives were particularly keen to buy red cloth. But fighting soon arose between the two parties, and even though the newcomers won the first battle with the help of their sharp iron weapons, they realised that "despite everything the land had to offer there, they would be under constant threat of attack from its prior inhabitants. They made ready to depart for their own country." So they returned to Straumsfjord and stayed there for a while.

Later that summer Karlsefni and some of his men set out to look for Thorhall the Hunter and his men, who had left the main party (cf. below). "They sailed north around Kjalarnes point and then westward of it, keeping the land on their port side. They saw nothing but wild forest. When they had sailed some distance they reached a river flowing from east to west. They sailed into the mouth of the river and lay near to the south bank."

It is difficult to tell where on the west coast of Newfoundland this place was. Here the newcomers again had trouble with the native inhabitants and Thorvald, son of Eirik the Red, was killed. So "they returned to spend their third winter in Straumsfjord. Many quarrels arose, as the men who had no wives sought to take those of the married men. Karlsefni's son Snorri was born there the first autumn and was three years old when they left."

Home to Iceland.
The next summer Karlsefni and his company left Vinland and, after one winter's stay in Greenland, he went home to Iceland with his wife Gudrid and their son Snorri. "He came home to his farm at Reynines. His mother thought his match hardly worthy and Gudrid did not stay there on the farm the first winter. But when she learned what an outstanding woman this was Gudrid moved to the farm and the two women got along well."
As already mentioned, among the descendants of Karlsefni and Gudrid were three distinguished Icelandic bishops of the twelfth century.

From 1999-2001 and in 2004 Jonas Kristjansson traveled around Newfoundland in search of Nordic artifacts. In the first three expeditions he traveled with the archaeologist Bjarni F. Einarsson, who acted as scientific advisor and expedition supervisor. Here is Bjarni on the scene in the wilderness of Newfoundland.

SOME VINLAND QUESTIONS.

Informants. Consonance and dissonance.
Here above the expedition of Thorfinn Karlsefni has been traced according to Eirik's Saga, without reference to Greenlanders' Saga, and it turns out that the account fits well with the geography and

local conditions in these western territories. However, some of the details are inaccurate and there is also much that is exaggerated. Eirik's Saga ends with the return of Karlsefni and Gudrid to Iceland and it is reasonable to conclude that the true essence of the stories lies in their accounts of the remarkable lives of these two.

One would expect that the accounts in Greenlanders' Saga would also have their roots in the tales of Karlsefni and Gudrid. In fact there is a direct reference to Karlsefni at the end of this saga. "It was Karlsefni who gave the most extensive reports of anyone of all of these voyages, some of which have now been set down in writing," says the saga.

Even if the accounts of events in Greenlanders' Saga are attributed to Karlsefni, he and Gudrid are not the main characters of the story in the same way as they are in Eirik's Saga. The comparison of the sagas that has been made above also indicates that Eirik's Saga not only gives a more detailed account but also comes closer to the truth in its account of the couple.

There are many important points on which the sagas are in agreement (cf. pp. 14-15 above). First and foremost is the genealogy: the names of the majority of the characters and their family relationships. Secondly, there are the names of new territories and their characteristics: Greenland, Helluland, Markland and Vinland; likewise some place names in Greenland and Vinland, such as Eiriksfjord, Brattahlid and Kjalarnes.

However, when it comes to the description of the events, the sagas are rarely in full agreement. The characters change roles, accounts of the same events are inconsistent and many events are only mentioned in one of the sagas. But this is exactly as one would expect when the stories have been passed on by word of mouth and then recorded by writers who put their own mark on the tale. As examples of different accounts of the same events may be mentioned Leif's rescue of the shipwrecked people; the unsuccessful Vinland expeditions of the two brothers Thorvald and Thorstein; the wonders in Lysufjord, etc.

One voyage to Vinland took place after the return of Karlsefni and Gudrid to Iceland: the disastrous journey of Freydis Eiriksdottir. It seems likely, although one cannot be sure, that both Karlsefni and Gudrid knew of this voyage. Moreover, if this tale was passed on with the others, the author of Eirik's Saga did not find it appropriate to put it into writing, but the author of Greenlanders' Saga knows not only about the journey but also about its consequences.

In Vinland Freydis committed the worst atrocity possible. She killed off the entire crew, men and women alike, of those who had joined her on the voyage. When Leif, her brother, discovered this terrible deed, he said: "I am not the one to deal my sister Freydis the punishment she deserves, but I predict that their descendants will not get on well in this world," the saga tells us. "As things turned out, after that no one expected anything but evil from them."

The discovery and exploration of Vinland.
Above, the possibility has been left open that both Bjarni Herjolfsson and Leif Eiriksson lost their way and thus reached Vinland or America. Little needed to go wrong for sailors on their way to Greenland to pass its southernmost point – and then it was inevitable that they would hit upon America. All things considered, the most reasonable explanation is to assume that these two men discovered the countries independently.

In an account passed down orally one would not expect to find two separate discoveries of Vinland. When Leif did not receive recognition for discovering Vinland in Greenlanders' Saga it was natural to give him the role of the explorer. This part has been taken from the account of Karlsefni´s expedition that can be found in Eirik´s Saga as has been described above.

Self-sown wheat.
Many theories have been advanced concerning the self-sown wheat said to have been found in Vinland. Some have claimed that this is

Bjarni and Jonas on the coast of the Bay of Exploits in the fall of 1999, searching for traces of Karlsefni's huts.

nothing more than a fairy tale, echoing the dreams in ancient and medieval times of the existence of a paradise island somewhere outside the known world. Adam of Bremen's account bears the mark of such ideas, but in later years it has often been the case that people have tried to find some domestic plant that can fulfil the conditions needed to confirm the accounts of Eirik's Saga and Greenlanders' Saga. For a long time the likely explanation was that this self-sown wheat referred to wild rice (*Zizania palustris*), which has been an important part of the Indian diet for thousands of years. It grows, among other places, in Nova Scotia, but there are no records of its having thrived in Newfoundland. But now a new theory has been put forward, that the self-sown wheat does not refer to wild rice but rather to wild rye (*Elymus virginicus*). This theory has two advantages with respect to my own theory. Firstly, the wild rye can grow in many places in southern Canada, and secondly, it can resemble both wheat and barley as well as rye. Upon this subject one can refer to the excellent book by the Swedish scholar Mats G. Larsson, *Vinland det goda* (1999).

Vines and grapes.
The word *vínber* (literally "wine-berries") is correctly understood as grapes in the Icelandic sagas written in the 13th century. But if we go back to the year 1000, the fruits which Leif and Karlsefni called "wine-berries" might simply have been some of the delicious berries that still abound in Newfoundland today. In the Swedish and Danish languages "wine-berries" (*vinbär, vinbær*) are the fruits known in English as "currants" (either "black" or "red currants"), whereas the foreign "grapes" are in those Scandinavian languages called *druvor, druer* (from German *Trauben*). In Iceland, on the other hand, neither black nor red currants were found in ancient times; accordingly, the Icelanders could use the same word for both the Newfoundland berries and for the Latin *uva* (grape), which they called *vínber* when translating Christian literature which has so much to say about those heavenly fruits. The Danes and Swedes, as noted above, mainly used a German word for *uva* to avoid confusing it with the domestic *vinbær*. Attempts to identify Viking Age Vinland from Icelandic literary accounts written centuries later has led modern historians to seek Vinland farther to the south, where wild grapes are to be found.

I have discussed this theory of mine more closely in an article in the Icelandic newspaper *Morgunblaðið* in May 2001. Later I discovered that the instigator of the Newfoundland-Vinland theory, W.A. Munn himself, maintained that the *vinber* in the sagas were not grapes, but just some of the indigenous berries in Newfoundland. Among other things he says (Wineland Voyages, pp. 15-16):

Since the start of the 20th century, a theory has been proposed now and then that the berries associated with Vinland were not the fruits that are now called grapes, but rather one of the types of succulent berries that have from time immemorial grown on Newfoundland. The photograph shows squashberries, from which W.A. Munn believes Vinland derives its name.

"In the early translation *vinber* has always been translated as grapes, and that was the principal reason for the very interesting books that have been written selecting 'Martha's Vinyard' near Boston, as the locality where Leif erected his booths. It is a noted place for wild grapes, and is the most northerly spot in America where these wild grapes grow in any quantity. Professor Fernald, the noted herbalist of Harvard University . . . has written an exhaustive treatise on this subject, and has proven beyond all doubt that Wineberry and not Grapes is the proper translation. He traces the

North Harbour is located on the far western side of the Bay of Exploits. Expedition members went there first in a motorboat with Captain Harold Manuel from Botwood in 1999, and then again by land in a four-wheeler in the spring of 2001. North Harbour is sheltered and would have been an adequate site for a farmstead. But the archaeologist Bjarni, who used georadar to investigate the site in the later expedition, said that he could find no evidence of habitation by Nordic peoples there.

meaning of this word and classification of Wineberry, from historical ages. His conclusion on this subject is as follows: 'Considering these facts,' he states, 'it is most probable that Vinber of the Sagas was Vaccinium–Vitis–Idaea which bears in its specific name a 'token of its long confusion by early botanists of northern Europe with the grape, which as late as 1633 bore the folkname of Wineberry,' (locally known in Newfoundland as Partridge berries. Swedish name, Lingon berries. Norwegian name, Tyttebar). He mentions that possibly Vinber is a native currant.'

"Instead of going into a long preamble of the different kind of berries that grow in Newfoundland that would answer the description in one way and another as mentioned in the Sagas, I will say at once that the Wineberries that so delighted Tyrker were our well-known Squash-berries. They grow in profusion around Pistolet Bay, on the dry hilly ground where there are copses or shrubby woods. When you mention berries to a person who has resided in Pistolet Bay, he tells you at once that the bay is noted for its Squash-berries. The Squash-berry bush is a shrub with thin stem about four feet high. The berries grow in bunches, and when ripe are of a brilliant red color; they remain on the bush all the winter. They have a delicious tart taste, and the fruit of the berry is almost wholly juice and often made into wine. The flavor is even more perfect in the spring than in the autumn, but the berry withers away when the frost is gone. You can get them in the fall, winter and spring; in some years of course more plentiful than others, but you will find patches of these squash-berries in that vicinity where a good picker could easily fill a barrel in one day, so that there would be no difficulty whatever for Leif and his crew to fill the after-boat. This Squash-berry gives an exact description of the Vinber mentioned in the Sagas."

Chronology.
It is impossible to determine precisely when these events are supposed to have taken place according to Eirik's Saga. According to Heimskringla, king Olaf Tryggvason sent Leif the Lucky to christianize Greenland the same spring as he sent Gissur the White and Hjalti Skeggjason to Iceland, which happened in the year 1000 "according to the general count" (Book of the Icelanders, p. 67). This is the basis on which scholars date the discovery of Vinland to that year. They then combine the chronologies of the two sagas, Eirik's Saga and Greenlanders' Saga, and arrive at the conclusion that Karlsefni came to Greenland in 1002 and went to search for Vinland in 1003.

But the chronologies in the two sagas are unclear. Furthermore, they disagree; people gather details from whichever saga suits their purposes. I shall now present the unclear chronology of Eirik's Saga, which here as elsewhere in this essay forms the basis for the discussion.

Leif goes to Christianize Greenland at the request of Olaf Tryggvason, and discovers Vinland, in the year 1000 at the latest; for it is known from other sources that King Olaf falls at Svoldur in that year. Later, Thorstein Eiriksson goes with his father to "seek out the land which Leif had found." They are tossed about "at sea" the whole summer and come home to Brattahlid "when it was almost winter." The saga does not specify how much time had passed since Leif's discovery when this happened, but some time must have elapsed, although not many years, between the voyages. Thorstein and Gudrid Thorbjarnardottir then go to live in Lysufjord, and Thorstein dies there during the first winter. Gudrid goes to Brattahlid to live with Eirik, her father-in-law.

Thorfinn Karlsefni comes to Greenland one summer. He marries Gudrid the following winter. The next summer they go to Vinland and stay there for three winters. They then spend one winter in Greenland and return to Iceland the next summer.

In this account, five years are clearly indicated. One summer goes to the unsuccessful journey of Thorsteinn Eiriksson; the following winter he dies in Lysufjord. Karlsefni and Gudrid are in Vinland for three winters and finally spend one winter in Greenland.

However, two time periods are not specified: (1) the time which elapses from Leif's discovery to his brother's unsuccessful journey, and (2) the time from when Gudrid comes to Eiriksfjord until Karlsefni comes to Greenland. During that period, her father Thorbjorn dies, "and all his money went to Gudrid. Eirik invited her to live with them and saw that she was well provided for." Then the saga states only that "one summer" Karlsefni prepared his ship to go to Greenland. It seems likely that during these two unspecified intervals some time elapsed, perhaps on the order of four years. In that case, nine years would have elapsed from the time when Leif discovered Vinland until Karlsefni and Gudrid return to Iceland.

The greatest problem with trying to determine the chronology of Eirik's Saga has yet to be mentioned: the author of the saga had neither the inclination nor the ability to date its events with any precision. The same applies to almost all authors of the Sagas of Icelanders. The author of Eirik's Saga never mentions any date in general history as a reference point. Such a context is only obtained through comparison with other texts; that is the year 1000, as mentioned above. In Eirik's Saga we cannot expect complete precision as to how long events take, how much time elapses between the events, how long people stay at this or that place, etc. It is always difficult to determine the proper chronology of events which took place long ago, even if the intention is there. Ari the Wise himself, who tries his best and very cleverly to determine the chronology of ancient Nordic history, does not even know how long the missionary Thangbrand stayed in Iceland (immediately before 1000), but says only that he was there "a winter or two." (Book of the Icelanders, p. 65) How will it be, then, when there is no interest in precise chronology, as in Eirik's Saga and the Greenlanders' Saga? Are we likely to be able to determine whether Karlsefni remained in Vinland for three years, as Eirik's Saga states, or perhaps only two, as the Greenlanders' Saga has it?

We know that Eirik the Red went to settle Greenland in 985 or 986 (Book of the Icelanders, p. 64). In Greenland there have been found many Christian graves of Nordic people but no pagan mounds; this shows that Christianity was brought there very early, probably around 1000 as in Iceland. Besides this, we can only say that the events which are recounted in the saga of Eirik the Red took place, according to that saga, before and after the millennium 1000, the last of them probably around 1010.

L'Anse aux Meadows. Vinland today

In 1914 an energetic businessman in St. John's, W.A. Munn (mentioned above), published a small pamphlet which he called *Wineland Voyages. The Location of Helluland, Markland and Vinland from the Icelandic Sagas*. Here he proposed for the first time that "Wineland the Good" was the same as the northernmost part of Newfoundland. At first his work received little attention. A new edition published in 1929 and more editions printed in the following years made the booklet better known, and in the mid-1940s and late 1950s an American engineer, A.H. Mallery, and the Danish archaeologist Jørgen Meldgaard gave Munn's thesis a timely fillip and provided further support for his theories. Then in 1959 the Norwegian explorer Helge Ingstad focused his attention on L'Anse aux Meadows, and in the 1960s the site was excavated under the expert leadership of his wife, the archaeologist Anne Stine Ingstad. Many Nordic turf-houses built for various purposes were discovered and also a smithy where the Vikings produced iron from sod and turned it into rivets and other crude but useful objects. In the 1970s further excavations on the site were conducted by the Canadian Parks Service, mostly under the direction of the archaeologist Birgitta Linderoth Wallace. In 1978 the ruins at L'Anse aux Meadows became the first archaeological site to be placed on the United Nations World Heritage List. A museum was founded with an exhibition where the artifacts discovered occupy a place of honour in the centre, and tourists flock to the place in spite of its isolated location.

Despite the fact that there are undoubtedly remains of Viking settlement at L'Anse aux Meadows, the place does not fit well into the accounts in the Icelandic sagas. Above we have traced the route of Karlsefni according to Eirik's Saga, and obviously he did not visit this place. This is supported by the archaeological investigations which find no traces of his diverse domestic livestock at L'Anse aux Meadows.

In some respects Greenlanders' Saga may be connected with L'Anse aux Meadows, but other characteristic features do not apply to the place: there was a river flowing from a lake into the sea, and they moved the ship "up into the river and from there into the lake, where they cast anchor" – this does not fit at all with L'Anse aux Meadows.

We have already seen that the sagas are inaccurate in many respects, which might provide the explanation for this discrepancy. It is a common experience all over the world that archaeological finds fit badly with written historical sources. In this case the reason might also be that the settlement was founded at a later point and that its construction did not take place until after our main informants, Karlsefni and Gudrid, had left for Iceland.

The location and characteristics of Vinland, naturally with a special focus on L'Anse aux Meadows, have been under constant investigation for the last decades and will probably be so far into the future. The theories of the numerous scholars have been quite varied. Helge Ingstad, partly in collaboration with his wife Anne Stine, published several books, the last one in the year 2000 when he was 101 years old. To the end he remained convinced that in L'Anse aux Meadows he had discovered the true and only Vinland. Other scholars locate Vinland farther to the southwest, at various places around the Gulf of St. Lawrence or elsewhere on the east coast of North America.

At first Helge Ingstad thought that the land had been named after the succulent berries that could be found there. Later, he adopted the views that a Swedish professor, Sven Söderberg, elaborated in a lecture delivered in 1898, and which were then published in a newspaper article in 1910. Söderberg suggested that the first element in the place name Vínland should be read *vin*, rather than *vín* (wine). In Old Norse the word *vin* means "grassland" or "pasture". The word appears in various Nordic place names, for instance in *Björgvin* (Bergen). A number of scholars found Söderberg's theory favorable, including Ingstad, who was convinced ever afterward that the land

Expedition members in Newfoundland early in May 2000: Jan Norman, archaeologist and photographer; Bjarni F. Einarsson, archaeologist; Kristjan Jonasson, assistant and photographer; Jan's wife, Liv Juhlin; and Jonas Kristjansson.

had been named *Vinland* in indication of the vast grassland of L'Anse aux Meadows. This denomination, however, must be considered entirely unthinkable. Linguists have contested it using secure proofs; see for instance Einar Haugen (1981). Icelanders have never confused *i* and *í*, *vin* and *vín*. The name *Vínland* has unshakeable roots in the traditions and literature of Iceland.

Birgitta Wallace not only led the final excavation at L'Anse aux Meadows and then organized and directed the Viking museum there; she has also been very active in publicizing the results of the extensive investigations. She has given numerous lectures, written popular articles, organized seminars and conferences and published collections of lectures and papers by other scholars. I shall now try to sum up in a few words the scholarly conclusions which may be said to represent the received view of today:

Around the year 1000 several expeditions were undertaken from Iceland and Greenland to thitherto unknown lands farther to the west. The explorers visited areas at least as far south as the southern part of the Gulf of St. Lawrence; this is proved by their discovering (wild) grapes and bringing back butter-nuts, which do not grow further north than that region.

The explorers could not determine their longitude, and therefore they had to sail by way of Helluland and Markland. Helluland would have been in the Canadian Arctic above the 58th parallel, most likely on Baffin Island. Markland must have lain within the confines of what is now Labrador. Because of the ice, ships could not have entered the Davis Strait much before the beginning of July, so the Vinland-farers would have had only two months at their disposal for exploration and collecting. Therefore they had to establish a winter camp at L'Anse aux Meadows on the northernmost point of modern Newfoundland, as a base for exploration and exploitation of resources farther south. At the camp they built turf-houses which could provide shelter for 70-90 persons. They also made a forge and smithy for producing bog iron and making artifacts, such as nails or rivets for repairing their ships.

The buildings have all been dated to the same period, around the year 1000. The occupation cannot have lasted long, only a few years, which is clearly indicated by the almost complete absence of accumulated garbage.

There are no byres, animal pens or corrals at L'Anse aux Meadows, which proves that the explorers had no intention of making a permanent settlement.

I myself have approached the Vinland problem, not as an archaeologist, but only as a critical saga scholar. From my modest point of view

I find the words of Birgitta Wallace and her "school" fully convincing. In the following I only wish to make a few additional remarks to their conclusions:

a. The name Vinland (Wineland) might simply have originated from the delicious berries abundant in Newfoundland. The Vikings might have called those fruits *vínber* (wine-berries).

b. The lack of any traces of animal husbandry at L'Anse aux Meadows seems to prove that Karlsefni did not try to settle down there. He did not even visit the place according to Eirik's Saga.

c. In his first fumbling expedition Karlsefni would have followed the coastlines as described in his saga. But after the explorers had got aquainted with the location of the new lands they would have sailed directly from Greenland to Labrador or to Newfoundland. Then they would have had far more than the two months allotted by Birgitta Wallace for exploration and collecting during each summer, even if they had come all the way from Greenland.

d. Birgitta Wallace and other scholars assume that all of the numerous houses at L'Anse aux Meadows were in use at the same time. She makes a rough estimate of the number of people in each house and arrives at the total sum of c. 70-90. (B.W. 2000, pp. 210- 211.) But it is not certain that all the houses were in use at the same time. In the so-called "Farm beneath the Sand" in the Western Settlement more than 30 rooms have been identified and it has been proven that they were not all in use at the same time. The old and dilapidated house was abandoned when the new one was built. (Joel Berglund 2000, pp. 295-303.) In this place the difference in age was so great that it could be determined by radiocarbon dating, which cannot be done at L'Anse aux Meadows where the houses are very much of the same age. But there two of the halls were burned down, and they are sufficiently far apart that an accidental fire would probably not have spread from one to the other. My guess is that people would only have lived in one or, at most, two of the big halls at any given time. One hall is burned, another is built and takes over; this house is also consumed by fire and then the third and last is erected. If the succession was thus we need only assume

43

a moderate number of explorers at the same time, not as many as 90 people as Birgitta Wallace claims. (B.W. 2000, p. 227.)

e. In recent times the location of Vinland has been the subject of much discussion. It has been placed almost everywhere between Virginia in the south and Labrador in the north. The most popular guesses today are the areas south of the Gulf of St. Lawrence (Nova Scotia, New Brunswick or Quebec). Earlier Birgitta Wallace did not find it possible to equate northern Newfoundland with Vinland. In her much-quoted article of 1986 she says (p. 300): "All scattered references to Vinland make it plain that, compared with Markland, Vinland was more bountiful, the weather was warmer, the tides were higher, the resources more exotic, and, above all, more varied." The butter-nuts and the grapes then offered the final proof.

In later years, on the other hand, Birgitta Wallace has tended not to demarcate Vinland too precisely. "Vinland is a region," she maintains; "L'Anse aux Meadows is merely a place in Vinland. Grapes grew at Hóp in southern Vinland; L'Anse aux Meadows was at the northern edge of Vinland, its port and entry." (B.W. 2000, p. 215.) All the same, I myself believe that Leif Eiriksson had in mind a definite place and definite country when he discovered a new land and named it *Vínland* (Wineland). And I believe, like W.A. Munn in the old days, that Wineland was the country which nowadays is called Newfoundland. In this land the explorers built their main headquarters, and then sailed from there to more southern and fertile lands, which may possibly have been given the same beautiful name.

However, the question of the whereabouts of Vinland apparently goes all the way back to the times of exploration. In Eirik's Saga itself, doubts are raised as to whether the explorers came to the "correct" Vinland. Actually the saga tells us explicitly that when the Scottish couple who were with Karlsefni came back from their exploration inland, one of them had "grapes in hand" and the other "self-sown wheat"; and in Hop "they found … vines growing on the hills." But all the same, one member of the party, Thorhall the Hunter, makes a verse

Jan and Bjarni preparing for an aerial survey in Botwood, May 1, 2000. In the photograph are Jonas, Liv, Bjarni, Jan, and the pilot, who is preparing his aircraft.

where he complains that he had been promised the best of drinks, but instead of these he was compelled to drink water: "No sweet wine do I sup, stooping at the spring." Accordingly, Thorhall wanted to seek Vinland farther to the south. He attempted to sail to the west of Kjalarnes, "but they ran into storms and were driven ashore in Ireland, where they were beaten and enslaved." Here as elsewhere the geography of the saga fits well with Newfoundland. We may doubt the exact truth of the account, but it seems that the verse was in any case composed by a disappointed man who did not believe that he had come to the real Wineland. It seems likely that he was in the company of Karlsefni, so that those contemporary verses would carry more weight

Bjarni uses his georadar in the search for artifacts in the spring of 2001, in a spot that looked hopeful according to aerial photographs. Jonas peers at the monitor expectantly.

than the fabulous younger narrative about the Scottish couple. And if there was already a disagreement among the first explorers concerning the location and properties of Vinland, it does not seem to be any disgrace for us moderns if we are unable to solve this mystery.

In the wake of Thorfinn Karlsefni

During the last few years I have undertaken four expeditions from Iceland to Newfoundland for the purpose of discovering the location of Keel Point and Wonder Beaches, Stream Bay and Hop. My main Icelandic assistants on the first three expeditions were my two sons,

Reg Hemeon drives Jonas on his four-wheeler from Fortune Harbour east to North Harbour in the spring expedition, 2001. Concerning this trip Jonas wrote in his journal: "The trip proved to be most gruelling, and the mud splattered up to my knees. Tree-trunks and planks had been laid in many places over trenches and other difficult patches of ground, and some spots were nearly impassable. The seat beneath me was a board hard as rock. I held on as tightly as I could to the boxes that were fastened onto the wheel-covers and supported myself on Reg's feet, as he steered his four-wheeler with great agility over and through trenches, hillocks, and pools of mud." — After arriving at North Harbour Bjarni ran his georadar over the area near the shore here and there, but found no traces whatsoever of ancient human dwellings (see also the photograph on page 35).

Gunnlaugur Jónasson and Kristján Jónasson and, most importantly, the Icelandic archaeologist Bjarni F. Einarsson, a learned and creative scholar. We made our headquarters in Botwood and our principal local assistants were Mr. Reginald Hemeon and Mr. Edward Evans. All of my expeditions have enjoyed the support of the Icelandic Ministry of Culture and of Icelandair.

Jonas and Thordur Ingi on the steps below the exhibition center at L'Anse aux Meadows during the fourth expedition, July 2004. It was around 25 degrees (Celsius) and the huge plain was luxuriant with grass.

In the autumn of 1999 we undertook preliminary research, driving through the east of Newfoundland, investigating in particular the surroundings of the Bay of Exploits but also looking briefly at other places, such as Hall's Bay and Gambo Pond. My assistants were Bjarni and Gunnlaugur. For two or three days we enjoyed the assistance of Capt. Harold Manuel of Gover's Harbor, visiting some places inaccessible by car.

In the spring of 2000 the group set out again, this time assisted by a Swedish archaeologist and photographer, Mr. Jan Norman. With the generous help of Ed and Reg, I secured the use of some aeroplanes, thereby enabling Jan and Bjarni to make three or four flights and undertake aerial photography of Gambo Pond, Bay of Exploits, Hall's Bay, White Bay, etc.

The third expedition was carried out in the spring of 2001; my assistants were Bjarni and my son Kristjan. This time Bjarni had acquired a modern archaeological aid, a so-called georadar, which he and Kristjan applied to potentially promising locations identified by Bjarni and Jan the previous summer.

During this trip we made the acquaintance of many fine and helpful individuals. Among them may be mentioned Mr. Lloyd Ryan of Lewisporte, who has since carried on an interesting correspondence with me, and also Dave Curran and Lloyd Noseworthy, generous helpers who granted me invaluable assistance in investigating the banks of Gambo Pond.

Unfortunately, it must be admitted that these three expeditions were not entirely successful. Indeed this is what might have been expected. My goal has been likened to searching for a needle in a haystack; however, there are many means of finding this needle.

It must be kept in mind that, according to Eirik's Saga, Karlsefni stayed in Vinland for three years with a large group of followers and "all kinds of livestock." To shelter all these people and creatures they must have built at least three houses in Straumsfjord and likewise in Hop. From all these activities there are bound to be many remains, as yet undiscovered.

Accordingly, the next sensible step was to mobilize various collaborators in Newfoundland and to form a kind of network covering the north-eastern part of the country. This I began on my fourth and last expedition, which was undertaken in July last summer, 2004. My only assistant on this trip was a young saga scholar, Thordur Ingi Gudjonsson. I was able to meet with most of my old friends and helpers and enjoyed the company of new friends with whom I had perviously only corresponded. At Gambo I met Mr. Mario Meeuwenoord, an energetic young Dutchman resident there. Particularly worth mentioning is Mr. Calvin Evans, a retired librarian from McGill University, now living at his old homestead in Botwood. Since I made his acquaintance he has given me much clever advice and invaluable assistance.

During my trip I supplied the enthusiasts with a set of photographs of Viking objects of the kind likely to have been left behind by Karlsefni's expedition, such as two axes, three swords, a spear, a brooch, a stone lamp, a ring-headed pin, a spindle whorl (specimens of the three last items were found at L'Anse aux Meadows), etc. If any such Nordic objects are discovered, their finding place may point the way to the ruins of Karlsefni's houses.

It is important that all possible discoverers obey the provisions of the Historic Resources Act, protecting archaeological sites and artifacts, set by the Government of Newfoundland and Labrador, Department of Tourism, Culture and Recreation, which declare i.a.:

"Should any archaeological remains be encountered, such as stone, bone or iron tools, concentrations of bone, charcoal or burned rock, fireplaces, house pits and/or foundations, activity in the area of the find must cease immediately and contact should be made with the Provincial Archaeologist in St. John's (729-2462) as soon as possible."

The enthusiasm I have raised has already produced considerable results. During my trip people showed me various objects which might be Viking and which they had discovered, sticking up from the earth or dug up from the foundation of a house. Such objects will in time be closely examined by archaeologists. And at present I feel optimistic: I have the impression that we may already have found, or in any case will find in the near future, some traces left by Karlsefni and Gudrid in their promised land.

BIBLIOGRAPHY

Adam of Bremen 1959. *History of the Archbishops of Bremen.* Translated with an Introduction and Notes by Francis J. Tschan. New York: Columbia University Press.

Book of the Icelanders (Íslendingabók) 1930. Edited and translated by Halldór Hermannsson. *Islandica* XX. Ithaca, New York: Cornell University Press.

Crozier, Allan 1998. The *Vinland Hypothesis. A Reply to the Historians. *Gardar* 29.

Eirik the Red's Saga 1997. *The Complete Sagas of Icelanders* I. General Editor Viðar Hreinsson. Reykjavík: Leifur Eiríksson Publishing.

Gathorne-Hardy, M. 1921. *The Norse Discoverers of America.* Oxford: Clarendon Press.

Gísli Sigurðsson 2000. The Quest for Vinland in Saga Scholarship. In *Vikings: North Atlantic Saga.*

Gísli Sigurðsson 2002. *Túlkun Íslendingasagna í ljósi munnlegrar hefðar.* Reykjavík: Stofnun Árna Magnússonar á Íslandi. English translation 2004: *The Medieval Icelandic Saga and Oral Tradition.* Cambridge, Mass. & London, England: The Milman Parry Collection of Oral Literature, Harvard University.

Greenlanders' Saga (or The Saga of the Greenlanders) 1997. *The Complete Sagas of Icelanders* I. General Editor Viðar Hreinsson. Reykjavík: Leifur Eiríksson Publishing.

Halldór Hermannsson 1936. The Problem of Wineland. *Islandica* 25. Ithaca, New York: Cornell University Press.

Haugen, Einar 1981. Was Vinland in Newfoundland? *Proceedings of the Eighth Viking Congress, Århus 24-31 August 1977.* Odense University Press.

Helgi Þorláksson 2001. The Vinland Sagas in Contemporary Light. *Approaches to Vinland.* Reykjavík: Stofnun Sigurðar Nordals.

Hermann Pálsson 2000. Vinland Revisited. *Northern Studies* 35.

Holm, Gösta 1997. Vinland 'Vinrankornas land'. *Gardar* 28.

Hovgaard, William 1914. *The Voyages of the Norsemen in America.* New York: The American Scandinavian Foundation.

Ingstad, Anne Stine 1985. *The Norse Discovery of America* I. Oslo: Norwegian University Press.

Ingstad, Helge 1966: *Land Under the Polestar.* New York: St. Martin Press.

Ingstad, Helge 1985. *The Norse Discovery of America* II. Oslo: Norwegian University Press.

Ingstad, Helge and Anne Stine 2000. *The Viking Discovery of America. The Excavation of a Norse Settlement in L'Anse aux Meadows, Newfoundland.* St. John's: Breakwater.
Islandske Annaler, ed. Gustav Storm 1888. Christiania: Det norske historiske Kildeskriftfond.
Íslendingabók, see *Book of the Icelanders*.
Jansson, Valter 1951. *Nordiska Vin-namn. En ortnamnstyp och dens historia.* Lund.
Jones, Gwyn 1986. *The Norse Atlantic Saga. Being the Norse Voyages of Discovery and Settlement to Iceland, Greenland, and North America.* A New and Enlarged Edition, with Contributions by Robert McGee, Thomas H. McGovern and colleagues, and Birgitta Linderoth Wallace. Oxford, New York: Oxford University Press.
Jón Jóhannesson 1956. Aldur Grænlendinga sögu. *Nordæla.* Reykjavík: Helgafell. English translation: The Date of the Composition of the Saga of the Greenlanders. *Saga Book* 16 (1962).
Jónas Kristjánsson 2001. Vínland Þorfinns Karlsefnis og Guðríðar Þorbjarnardóttur. *Lesbók Morgunblaðsins 5. maí og 12. maí.* Reykjavík.
Jónas Kristjánsson 2004. The Good Wineland. *The Advertiser, April 15.* Grand Falls – Windsor, Newfoundland.
Knirk, James E. 1997. Kensington Runestone. *Scandinavian Studies* 69.
Larsson, Mats G. 1999. *Vinland det goda. Nordbornas färder till Amerika under vikingatiden.* Stockholm: Atlantis.
Lönnroth, Erik 1996. The Vinland Problem. *Scandinavian Journal of History* 21.
Magnús Stefánsson 1997. Vínland eller Vinland? *Festskrift til Historisk institutts 40-års jubileum 1997.* Bergen.
Mallery, A.H. 1951. *Lost America. The Story of Iron-Age Civilization prior to Columbus.* Washington D.C.: Overlook Co.
Matthías Þórðarson 1929. Vínlandsferðirnar. *Safn til sögu Íslands* VI. Reykjavík: Hið íslenzka bókmenntafélag. English translation: *The Vinland Voyages.* New York 1930.
Morison, Samuel Elliot 1971-74. *The European Discovery of America. The Northern Voyages.* New York: Oxford University Press.
Munn, W.A. 1914. *Wineland Voyages. The Location of Helluland, Markland and Vinland from the Icelandic Sagas.* St. John's: The Evening Telegram Limited. Here quoted from the 1946 edition, facsimiled in 1992.
Ólafur Halldórsson 1978. *Grænland í miðaldaritum.* Reykjavík: Sögufélag.

Páll Bergþórsson 1997. *Vínlandsgátan.* Reykjavík: Mál og menning.

Páll Bergþórsson 2000. *The Wineland Millennium. Saga and Evidence.* Reykjavík: Mál og menning.

Rafn, Carl Christian 1837. *Antiquitates Americanæ sive scriptores septentrionales rerum ante-Columbianarum in America.* Havniæ: Societas regia antiquariorum septentrionalium.

Vikings: The North Atlantic Saga. Edited by William W. Fitzhugh and Elisabeth I. Ward 2000. Washington and London: Smithsonian Institution Press.

Vinland Revisited. The Norse World at the Turn of the First Millennium. *Selected Papers from the Viking Millennium International Symposium, 15-24 September 2000.* Edited by Shannon Lewis-Simpson.

Wallace, Birgitta Linderoth 1986. The L'Anse aux Meadows Site. In Jones, Gwyn. *The Norse Atlantic Saga.*

Wallace, Birgitta Linderoth 1991a. L'Anse aux Meadows. Gateway to Vinland. *Acta Archaeologica*, Vol. 61. Copenhagen.

Wallace, Birgitta Linderoth 1991b. The Vikings in North America: Myth and Reality. *Social Approaches to Viking Studies.* Ed. Ross Samson. Glasgow: Cruithne Press.

Wallace, Birgitta Linderoth 1993. L'Anse aux Meadows, the Western Outpost. *Viking voyages to North America.* Ed. Birthe L. Clausen. Roskilde: Viking Ship Museum.

Wallace, Birgitta Linderoth 2000a. The Viking Settlement at L'Anse aux Meadows. In *Vikings: The North Atlantic Saga.*

Wallace, Birgitta Linderoth 2000b. An Archaeologist's Interpretation of the *Vinland Sagas.* In *Vikings: The North Atlantic Saga.*

Wallace, Birgitta Linderoth and Fitzhugh, William W. 2000. Stumbles and Pitfalls in the Search for Viking America. In *Vikings: The North Atlantic Saga.*